Nap in it

Written by Caroline Green

Collins

Nap in it.

Sip it.

sip

Sip it.

sip

Pat it.

pads

pat pat

tip

Sit in it.

sit

Dip in it.

dip

Nip at it.

nip nip

tip

It is dim.

nap nap nap

🐾 After reading 🐾

Letters and Sounds: Phase 2

Word count: 38

Focus phonemes: /s/ /a/ /t/ /p/ /i/ /n/ /m/ /d/

Curriculum links: Understanding the world

Early learning goals: Reading: read and understand simple sentences; use phonic knowledge to decode regular words and read them aloud accurately

Developing fluency

- Your child may enjoy hearing you read the book.
- Encourage your child to read the left-hand pages, encouraging them to pause after full stops. Remind them to read any labels too.

Phonic practice

- Turn to page 9 and point to the word **Dip**. Ask your child to sound out and blend the letters in the word. (*d/i/p* – **dip**)
- On pages 12 and 13, focus on **dim**. Ask your child to sound out and blend it. (*d/i/m* – **dim**) Can they spot sounds that are the same or different in **dip** and **dim**?
- Look at the "I spy sounds" pages (14 and 15). Point to and sound out the /m/ at the top of page 14, then point to the map and say "map", emphasising the /m/ sound. Can your child spot other things that start with the /m/ sound? (e.g. *man, mug, mountain, monkey, meerkats, mouse, mask, medal*)

Extending vocabulary

- Turn to pages 4 and 5 and reread the text. Ask your child: What word could you use instead of **sip**? (e.g. *drink, lap*) Talk about the meanings of **sip** and lap, and how they explain certain ways in which animals can drink.
- Talk about words to do with drinking, e.g. *guzzle, gulp, swallow, suck*.